PROFESSOR COOK'S FRUITY DESSERTS

Enslow Publishers, Inc.
40 Industrial Road
Box 398
Berkeley Heights, NJ 07922
USA

http://www.enslow.com

This edition published by Enslow Publishers Inc.

Library of Congress Cataloging-in-Publication Data:

Brash, Lorna.
  Professor Cook's Fruity Desserts / Lorna Brash.
    pages cm. — (Professor Cook's ...)
  Audience: 9-12
  Audience: Grade 4 to Grade 6
  Summary: "A variety of recipes for desserts made with fruit.
Each also has a science bit which explains how the dessert comes together"—Provided by publisher.
  Includes bibliographical references.
  ISBN 978-0-7660-4302-2
  1. Desserts—Juvenile literature. 2. Cooking—Juvenile literature. I.Title. II. Series.
        TX773.S3547 2013
        641.86—dc23

                                                    2012031115

Future edition:
  Paperback ISBN: 978-1-4644-0549-5

To Our Readers:
We have done our best to make sure all Internet addresses in this book were active and appropriate when we went to press. However, the author and the publisher have no control over and assume no liability for the material available on those Internet sites or on other Web sites they may link to. Any comments or suggestions can be sent by e-mail to comments@enslow.com or to the address on the back cover.

Printed in China

012013 WKT, Shenzhen, Guangdong, China

10 9 8 7 6 5 4 3 2 1

First published in the UK in 2012 by Wayland

Copyright © Wayland 2012

Wayland
338 Euston Rd
London NW1 3BH

Editor: Debbie Foy
Designer: Lisa Peacock
Photographer: Ian Garlick
Proofreader/indexer: Sarah Doughty
Consultant: Sean Connolly

Wayland is a division of Hachette Children's
Books, an Hachette UK company.
www.hachette.co.uk

Contents

PROFESSOR COOK'S... INCREDIBLE EDIBLES

Are you hungry to learn more about your food?

Have you ever wondered why some foods behave the way they do? For example, have you ever considered how jellies or mousses set into their amazing wobbly shape? Or how a chocolate dip stays runny instead of setting hard?

Have you ever wondered what happens when fruit is frozen or how bananas can help ripen other fruit? Why we need to eat 5 servings of fruits and vegetables a day or even how yogurt contains friendly bacteria?

You can find the answers to these questions and more by joining Professor Cook's team to make instant frozen yogurt, hot pineapple "lollies", strawberry mousse with the wobble factor or tropical fruit with goo-ey chocolate dip!

Happy ~~Experimenting~~ Cooking!

PROFESSOR COOK'S KITCHEN RULE BOOK

→ Wash your hands before you start cooking and after handling raw stuff, like meat

→ Mop up spills as soon they happen

→ Use oven gloves for handling hot dishes straight from the oven

→ Take care with sharp knives. Don't walk around with them!

→ Turn off the oven or stovetop when you have finished cooking

→ Use separate cutting boards for vegetables and meat

→ Store raw and cooked foods separately in the fridge

→ Don't forget to tidy up the kitchen afterwards! No-brainer, huh?

Abbreviations

c = cup

tsp = teaspoon

tbsp = tablespoon

oz = ounce

°F = degree Fahrenheit

HOT GOODS!

WHEN YOU SEE THIS WARNING SIGN AN ADULT'S HELP MAY BE NEEDED!

The "Science Bits"

Believe it or not, cooking involves a lot of science! The Science Bits that accompany each of Professor Cook's delicious recipes answer all the mysteries about food that you have ever wanted to know. They also explore some of the interesting, unusual or quirky ways that our food often behaves!

TROPICAL FRUIT WITH GOO-EY CHOCOLATE DIP

Rich with choccy-ness, this dip is the perfect complement to fresh and tangy tropical fruits. But what makes the dip stay goo-ey enough for you and your pals to keep coming back for more (and more)?

Stuff you need:

2 kiwi fruit
1/4 fresh pineapple
8 strawberries
1 star fruit
1 tbsp lemon juice
1 large ripe mango
Juice of 1/2 lemon
8 tbsp runny honey
8 tbsp milk
8 tbsp heavy cream
8 oz dark chocolate, broken into squares

Serves 4

HOT GOODS

Step 1

Find 12 wooden skewers. Rinse all the fruit well.

Step 2

Peel the kiwi fruit and pineapple and cut into chunks. De-hull the strawberries. Slice the star fruit and brush with lemon juice. Cut a slice from either side of the mango and discard the stone. Cut a crisscross pattern into the flesh, turn inside out and cut away the mango cubes.

Step 3

Thread the fruit onto the pointed end of each skewer.

The star fruit is an excellent source of ascorbic acid (Vitamin C), important in keeping bones, teeth and skin healthy!

The Science Bit
What makes the chocolate stay runny?

Melted chocolate usually sets, agreed? It's an example of a reversible change because chocolate melts, sets solid, then melts again. But here, heavy cream, honey and milk are added. The fats in the cream and milk combine with the cocoa butter, a vegetable fat in the chocolate. This combo of fats can produce a (WARNING: science word coming up!) eutectic system, which, in simple terms, means the chocolate stays runny!

Step 4

Put the honey, milk, heavy cream and chocolate in a small saucepan and heat gently over a low heat, stirring continuously until melted. Pour into a small bowl and serve with the fruit skewers.

INCREDIBLE EDIBLE TIE-DYE ICE POPS

Who said you can only tie-dye clothes? Why not try ice pops instead! They are packed full of juicy blackberries all wrapped up in a creamy "brain-freezing" yogurt!

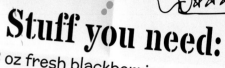

Stuff you need:

3 oz fresh blackberries

Finely grated rind and juice of 1 lemon

4 tbsp powdered sugar

10 oz vanilla or natural yogurt

Makes 4 ice pops

Step 1

Place the blackberries and 1 tbsp lemon juice into a bowl and mash with a fork.

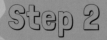
Step 2

Mix together the remaining lemon juice, lemon rind, powdered sugar and yogurt.

Blackberries are high in antioxidants called anthocyanins, which give them their dark color!

Step 3

Drop a few spoonfuls of yogurt mixture into 4 1/2 cup ice pop molds, then add a spoonful of blackberry mixture. Keep doing this until you have used up all the mixture and filled all the molds.

Step 4

Push a wooden skewer into each ice pop mold to stir up the mixtures a little. Cover the ice pop molds with their lids and freeze for at least 12 hours or overnight.

The Science Bit

What exactly __is__ brain freeze?

Brain freeze is the pain you feel when you eat freezing cold food such as ice cream. When the cold food touches the roof of your mouth it makes the blood vessels shrink, or constrict. The sharp pain that you can get is caused by the blood rushing back into the blood vessels in order to heat the blood up again. Luckily, brain freeze usually only lasts about 30 seconds!

ICY WATERMELON FRUIT SLICES

There's nothing more refreshing than a slice of watermelon on a hot summer's day. So why not try our icy watermelon sorbet version!

Stuff you need:

1 small watermelon, halved
1/3 c superfine sugar
1 medium egg white
1 c blueberries

Serves 8

Step 1

Scoop out the flesh from the watermelon halves leaving the shell intact. Roughly chop the flesh.

Step 2

Place the watermelon and sugar into a food processor and whizz to a slushy puree. Pour into a freezer-proof container and freeze for 4 hours until semi-frozen.

The Science Bit

Why add egg whites to sorbet?

Adding egg white to your sorbet help to give it a more creamy consistency and adds volume and texture. It also helps to stabilize the mixture (as an emulsifier). Emulsifying the mixture means that you can keep it in the freezer for longer!

Step 3

Use a fork to break up any large ice crystals. Whisk the egg white until stiff and fold into the frozen mixture. Add the blueberries. Spoon the semi-frozen mixture into one half of the watermelon shell. Cover with plastic wrap and freeze overnight. Remove from the freezer 20 minutes before serving.

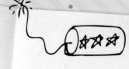

Stuff you need:

12 bamboo skewers
1 ripe pineapple, peeled
1/2 tbsp butter
1 tbsp light brown sugar
Finely grated rind of 1 lime
Chopped pistachio nuts (optional)

Makes 12

HOT GOODS!

Speed up the ripening of a pineapple by standing it upside down on its leafy end!

Sticky and really juicy, these caramelized hot "lollies" are even tastier when dipped in chopped pistachios!

Step 1

Soak the skewers in cold water for 25 minutes to stop them burning under the grill. Halve the pineapple lengthways and then cut each half into six long, thin wedges. Push each piece of pineapple onto a wooden skewer.

HOT PINEAPPLE "LOLLIES"

Step 2

Mix the butter, sugar and lime rind together to make a smooth paste.

Step 3

Heat a griddle pan until smoking and add the pineapple skewers. Cook for 2 minutes on each side until slightly charred. Dot the pineapple with the butter mixture and cook for a further minute until the sugar mixture has dissolved.

Step 4

Sprinkle with pistachio nuts if you like them, and serve warm.

The Science Bit
Why is pineapple a jelly's worst enemy?

While pineapple is a deliciously nutritious fruit packed with Vitamin C and fiber, it also contains an enzyme called bromelain, which acts to digest protein. So, if you add pineapple to a fruit jelly it simply won't set because the bromelain will act on the gelatin proteins and break them down!

SUPER BLUEBERRY CHEESECAKE

One slice will not be enough! Crisp on the bottom, refreshing and creamy in the middle and super fruity on the top. Triple wow!

Stuff you need:

2/3 c coconut cookies

1 1/2 tbsp butter

1 c superfine sugar

Finely grated rind and juice of 2 limes

2 1/4 c ricotta cheese or cottage cheese (drained)

1 1/4 c heavy cream

1/4 oz powdered gelatin

1 c fresh blueberries

Serves 8

Step 1

Break up the cookies and whizz in a food processor to make fine crumbs. Melt the butter in a saucepan and stir in the crumbs to coat evenly. Line the base of a 9 in springform cake pan with parchment paper. Press the cookie mixture firmly into the base of the pan. Chill for 10 minutes in the fridge.

Step 2

In a large bowl mix together half of the superfine sugar, lime zest and half the lime juice, ricotta cheese and heavy cream until well combined.

Step 3

Sprinkle the gelatin over 3 tbsp of warm water in a small bowl. Leave for 5 minutes. Place the bowl over a pan of hot water and heat until the gelatin has dissolved. Allow to cool for 5 minutes.

Step 4

Drizzle the dissolved gelatin into the creamy cheese mixture and whisk. Pour over the cookie base and chill for 2–3 hours until set.

Step 5

Place the remaining sugar, lime juice and blueberries into a saucepan and heat gently until the sugar has dissolved and the blueberries are just releasing their juice. Remove the cheesecake from its pan and pour over the blueberry sauce to serve.

The Science Bit

Why do we add lime?

Lime adds a sharp citrus flavor and its acidity is a good partner to a rich, creamy cheesecake. Plus, scientists believe that our taste buds sense some flavors more strongly if they are offset by other flavors. So, we appreciate the cheesecake even more because it is combined with sour lime!

WOBBLY STRAWBERRY MOUSSE

What is packed full of sweet and nutritious strawberries but is high on the wobble factor? It's our amazing strawberry mousse! Move over jelly...

Step 1

Brush the inside of a 2 1/2 cup gelatin mold with oil. Follow the directions on the gelatin package to add the correct amount of water.

Stuff you need:

1 tsp vegetable oil
1 tbsp plus 3/4 tsp gelatin
2 3/4 c strawberries, hulled and quartered
3/4 c powdered sugar
2 c heavy cream
Fresh strawberries and mint leaves, to decorate

Serves 6-8

Did you know? There are about 200 seeds in every strawberry!

Step 2

Place the strawberries and powdered sugar into a food processor and whizz to a smooth puree. Strain the strawberry mixture into a large bowl to create a smooth sauce.

Step 3

Gently warm the cream in a saucepan. Then add gelatin mixture. Stir until dissolved. Whisk in the strawberry puree, then pour into the gelatin mold. Chill overnight.

Step 4

Dip the sides of the gelatin mold into a bowl of warm water for about 30 seconds. Lift out of the water and cover with a plate. Turn the mold and the plate over and lift the mold away from the pudding. Decorate with fresh strawberries and mint.

The Science Bit

What creates the wobble factor?

It's gelatin! When heated gelatin becomes soluble, but when cooled it forms a gel. This gel acts as a kind of protein "mesh" that traps water from the other liquids present in the recipe. This is a reversible process, as the gelatin will melt on heating but when cooled will reform again.

"MAGIC" APPLE & BLACKBERRY PUDDING

Try this fabulously fruity pudding with a delicious sauce that appears — as if by magic!

Step 1

Preheat the oven to 375°F. Put the apples and blackberries into an ovenproof dish and sprinkle with 1/4 c of the sugar.

Step 2

Cream the butter and remaining sugar until pale and fluffy. Stir in the flour, lemon rind and juice, egg yolks and milk and beat until smooth. Don't worry if your mixture looks curdled!

Stuff you need:

2 c cooking apples, peeled, and cut into thick slices

1 c blackberries

3/4 c powdered sugar

1/2 tbsp softened butter

1/2 tbsp plain flour

Finely grated rind and juice of 1 lemon

2 medium eggs, separated

3/4 c milk

1 oz flaked almonds

Powdered sugar, to dust

Serves 6

HOT GOODS!

Step 3

Whisk the egg whites until stiff and fold them into the lemon mixture. Spoon over the fruit to cover. Sprinkle over the flaked almonds.

Step 4

Place the ovenproof dish into a large roasting pan and very carefully pour boiling water until it reaches halfway up the sides of the ovenproof dish. Transfer to the oven and bake for 45–50 minutes. Dust with powdered sugar and serve warm.

The Science Bit

What causes the "magic" sauce?

The magic sauce is the result of the ingredients being denatured (or changed) in a chemical reaction. It's the acid in the lemon juice that helps them change in different ways. The proteins in the eggs and milk break down and release air (causing the pudding mixture to rise) but the cell walls of the fruits break down, making them more liquid. And that's magic!

Stuff you need:

For the ice bowl:
Small handful blueberries
1 kiwi fruit, sliced
1 star fruit, sliced
4 Gerbera flower heads (Only eat flowers labeled safe for human consumption)
8 strawberries, halved
Handful ice cubes

For the fruit salad:
1 star fruit
1 lemon, halved
1/2 small melon, cut into chunks
1/2 c seedless red grapes
1 kiwi fruit, peeled and chopped
1/3 c canned mandarin oranges
1 small papaya, peeled and chopped
1/2 c white grape juice

Serves 4-6

Put on your gloves to make this wonderful icy creation to hold a tasty fruit salad. Brrrr...!

The Science Bit
What is dry ice?

Dry ice is NOT used in this recipe but it is still fascinating to know about! Dry ice is frozen carbon dioxide (CO_2) and is often used to preserve perishable items such as fruit. Fruits frozen with dry ice will thaw out to be firm instead of soggy or waterlogged!

ICE BOWL FRUIT SALAD

Step 1

For the ice bowl, fill a 2 1/2 quart glass mixing bowl two-thirds full with water. Place a 1 quart glass mixing bowl into the center of the water. Secure with sticky tape so that the smaller bowl is central and the rims are level. Push the fruit and flowers into the water. Add ice cubes to keep them submerged. Freeze overnight.

Step 2

For the fruit salad, carefully slice the star fruit and squeeze the lemon juice over it. Combine the melon, grapes, kiwi, and oranges with the papaya, star fruit, and grape juice. Chill until ready to use.

Step 3

Remove the bowls from the freezer. Fill the smaller one with warm water to ease it out. Turn the larger bowl over. Pour warm water over the back of the larger bowl until the ice bowl inside releases. Place it onto a serving plate, add the fruit salad and serve!

NICEY SLICEY SUMMER FRUIT JELLY

This summer jelly is jam-packed with fruity goodness. You will be well on your way to your 5 servings a-day!

Step 1

Add 1 c water to the sugar and heat gently in a pan, stirring until the sugar dissolves. Bring to a boil and boil rapidly for 1 minute. Add the apple and raspberry, and the lemon juices.

Raspberries come in many colors. There are black, purple and even golden raspberries!

Step 2

Soften the gelatin by following the directions on the package. Leave for 2–3 minutes. Stand the bowl over a pan of simmering water for 2–3 minutes until the gelatin dissolves. Then add the gelatin to the juice mixture and stir.

Step 3

Place the nectarines, raspberries and red currants into a 1 1/4-quart nonstick loaf pan and mix gently. Pour the gelatin mixture over the fruit to cover and allow to set overnight.

The Science Bit

What is your "5 a-day"?

Scientists have shown that eating at least 5 portions of fruit and vegetables each day has important health benefits and can help to prevent heart disease and some cancers. Fresh, frozen, dried and canned fruit and veg can count as part of your 5 servings a-day!

Step 4

To release the jelly from the loaf pan , carefully dip the tin into warm water for 30 seconds. Position a plate over the top of the jelly and quickly turn the plate over. Lift the loaf pan off. Ta-dah!

Stuff you need:

2 c whole milk
1/2 tbsp dried milk powder
3 tbsp "live" natural yogurt
1/3 c dried apricots, halved
1 tbsp raisins
1 tbsp dried cherries
1 fruit tea bag
1 split vanilla pod
1 red apple, cored and sliced
Runny honey, to serve

Serves 4

HOT GOODS!

Did you know that some yogurt is a living culture? Why not try making our homemade yogurt recipe for a totally wholesome breakfast?

Step 1

Place the milk and milk powder into a saucepan and whisk until well combined. Place over the lowest heat and allow to warm gently without boiling.

HOMEMADE YOGURT WITH FRUIT SQUISH

Step 2

Stir in the yogurt and pour into a thermos. Set aside and leave overnight until set.

Step 3

Place the fruit into a pan with the tea bag, vanilla pod and 3/4 c boiling water and leave to go cold.

Step 4

Drain the fruit, discard the tea bag and remove the vanilla pod. Very carefully remove the seeds from the pod and stir into the yogurt. Divide the yogurt between 4 glasses. Spoon over the soaked fruit and add apple slices. Drizzle with honey to serve.

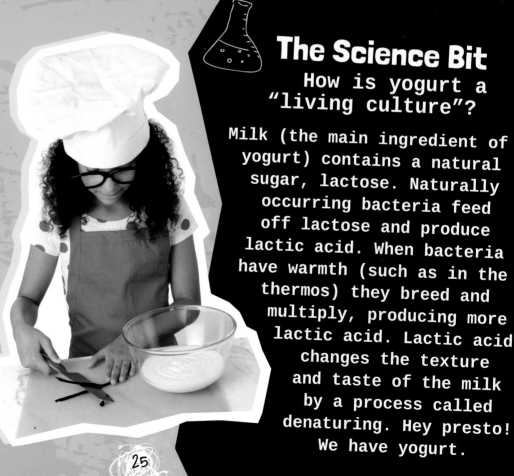

The Science Bit
HOW is yogurt a "living culture"?

Milk (the main ingredient of yogurt) contains a natural sugar, lactose. Naturally occurring bacteria feed off lactose and produce lactic acid. When bacteria have warmth (such as in the thermos) they breed and multiply, producing more lactic acid. Lactic acid changes the texture and taste of the milk by a process called denaturing. Hey presto! We have yogurt.

Stuff you need:

16 oz bag frozen mixed
summer fruit

1 3/4 c Greek yogurt

Finely grated rind and juice of
1 large orange

2 tbsp powdered sugar

Small handful fresh cherries

Mint sprigs, to decorate

Serves 6

Cherries are rich in melatonin which has a soothing and relaxing effect on the brain!

The Science Bit

Does freezing alter your fresh fruit?

Fresh fruit retains a lot of its nutrients if frozen quickly after picking. But fresh fruit tends to lose its shape when defrosted. This happens because the cells are broken when the water in them expands as it freezes. So frozen fruits are ideal for cooking or blending into recipes like frozen yogurt!

INSTANT FROZEN YOGURT

This ready-before-you-know-it frozen yogurt is a healthy alternative to ice cream since it contains half the fat and is stuffed full of healthy fruit!

Step 1

Place the frozen fruit, yogurt, orange rind, juice and powdered sugar into a food processor. Whizz up the mixture (using a spatula to scrape down the sides of the food processor) until totally smooth.

Step 2

Spoon the yogurt mixture into serving glasses. Top with fresh cherries and mint sprigs to serve.

STICKY LICKY BANOFFEE CONES

Whizz up an banana-licious treat in a cone! Bananas are healthy and taste good but they also have other very special uses.

Step 1

Peel 3 bananas and cut into thick slices. Arrange on a baking sheet and freeze for at least 2 hours until solid.

Step 2

While keeping the bananas frozen, peel and chop the remaining banana and push a quarter of it into each cone. Stand the cones upright in a measuring cup to help you. Add 1 tbsp of caramel sauce into each cone.

Step 3

Remove the bananas from the freezer and whizz up in a food processor with the vanilla, sugar, and half the buttermilk. Scrape down the sides using a spatula, add the remaining buttermilk and whizz again until smooth.

Step 4

Spoon the ice cream into the cones, top with dried banana, a drizzle of caramel sauce and dust with chocolate.

The Science Bit

How are bananas useful?

To speed up the ripening of fruits such as avocados, mangoes, peaches, and pears, place a ripe banana and the unripe fruit into a paper bag. The banana emits a gas called ethylene which acts as a signal to other fruit to start ripening. How useful is that?

PROFESSOR COOK'S GLOSSARY

ANTHOCYANINS pigments that give many fruits their dark color

ANTIOXIDANTS substances found in many fruits and vegetables that help to prevent damage in the body and repair cells

ASCORBIC ACID a form of vitamin C, mainly found in fruits and vegetables

BACTERIA single-celled organisms that are found in the air, in water, in food and many other places, some of which cause disease

BROMELAIN an enzyme found in pineapple and kiwi fruits that breaks down the protein, gelatin

BUTTERMILK a slightly sour liquid left after butter has been churned, often used in baking

CELLS tiny units that make up all living things

CULTURE the growth of organisms

DENATURING to remove or alter the natural qualities of something

EMULSIFY to create a mixture of two or more liquids (which would not normally mix)

ENZYMES molecules that control chemical reactions in living organisms

ETHYLENE a gas produced by bananas that causes other fruits to ripen

EUTECTIC this describes a mixture of chemical substances that melts at a lower temperature than either of the mixed substances

FIBER food items that add bulk to our diets such as cereals, fruits and vegetables

GEL a semi-solid material

GELATIN a setting agent used in many puddings and desserts

GRIDDLE PAN a heavy cast-iron pan that creates chargrilled "lines" across your food

HORMONE a chemical produced by living things that help make changes in cells

LACTIC ACID an acid present in sour milk and also produced in our muscles when we exercise

MELATONIN a hormone produced in the body that is involved in regulating the sleeping and waking cycles

NUTRIENTS these are substances found in our food and drink, including carbohydrates, minerals, proteins and vitamins

PRESERVATIVE substances added to food to prevent it from spoiling

REVERSIBLE CHANGE a chemical process that can be reversed (or turned back)

SOLUBLE describes substances that can be easily dissolved in a liquid

SPRINGFORM CAKE PAN a cake pan with removable sides and base

WHISK to beat with a light, rapid motion

INDEX

USEFUL WEBSITES

www.spatulatta.com
Get some basic cooking skills under your belt, with step-by-step video recipes and a recipe box that includes options for cooking a meal by choosing a basic ingredient, a type of food, occasion or particular diet.

www.yummyscience.co.uk
Super-fun science projects to try out in the kitchen using everyday foods. Grow your own crystals with salt, test out the toasting properties of bread or make your own honeycomb toffee. Some of these recipes call for an adult's help, so always make sure you let an adult know before you start.

www.exploratorium.edu/cooking
Find out how a pinch of curiosity can improve your cooking! Explore recipes, activities and webcasts that will improve your understanding of the science behind food and cooking.

Discover some more incredible edibles with Professor Cook and the team!

Professor Cook's Dynamite Dinners

978-0-7660-4301-5
Professor Cook's Incredible Edibles!
Sticky Chicky Burger Stacks
Tex-Mex
Taco Bowl Salad
Incredible Edible Bowl Soup!
Posh Fish 'n' Chips 'n' Dip!
Boost Your Burger!
Finger Lickin' Chicken Satay
Japan-Easy Tuna Rolls
Tongue-Tingling Sweet and Sour Noodles
Thirsty Couscous Cakes!
Scrambly Egg Fried Rice
Superfood Cannelloni
Chili with a Deep, Dark Secret
Professor Cook's Glossary
Index & Useful Web Sites

Professor Cook's Mind-Blowing Baking

978-0-7660-4303-9
Professor Cook's Incredible Edibles!
Crimson velvet whoopie pies!
Choccy choux puffs
Exploding cupcakes!
Squidgy widgy custard tarts
Oozing crust pizza
Very berry choco ripple meringues
Kitchen sink potpies
Hot ice cream sparkle
Super seedy flowerpot bread
Stack 'em high cheesy puff pie
Black & blue buns
Stained glass cookies
Professor Cook's Glossary
Index & Useful Web Sites

Professor Cook's Fruity Desserts

978-0-7660-4302-2
Professor Cook's Incredible Edibles!
Tropical fruit with goo-ey chocolate dip
Incredible edible tie-dye ice pops
Icy watermelon fruit slices
Hot pineapple "lollies"
Super blueberry cheesecake
Wobbly strawberry mousse
"Magic" apple & blackberry pudding
Ice bowl fruit salad
Nicey slicey summer fruit jelly
Homemade yogurt with fruit squish
Instant frozen yogurt
Sticky licky banoffee cones
Professor Cook's Glossary
Index & Useful Web Sites

Professor Cook's Smashing Snacks

978-0-7660-4304-6
Professor Cook's Incredible Edibles!
Pop-tastic popcorn
Smashing caramel shards
Ice cream in a bag
Cheese-and-ham-o-rama!
Homemade beans on toast
Oat-so yummy power cookies
"No-cry" onion bhajis & dip
Double-dipped mallow cookies
Mini superhero pies!
Gold bullion honeycomb bars!
Pink fizzbomb lemonade
Big dipper breadsticks
Professor Cook's Glossary
Index & Useful Web Sites